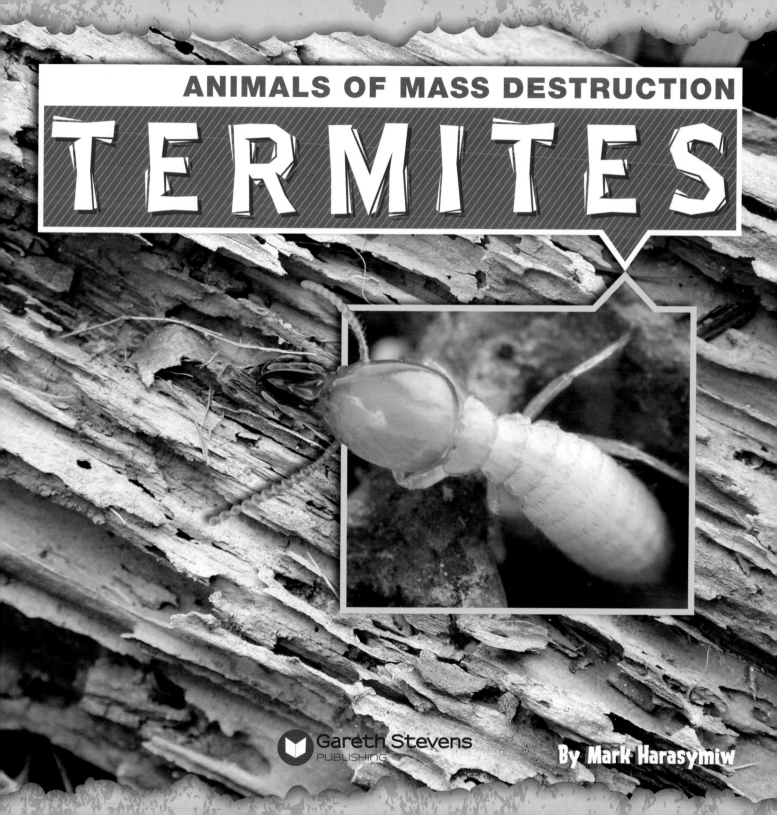

ANIMALS OF MASS DESTRUCTION

TERMITES

Gareth Stevens
PUBLISHING

By Mark Harasymiw

Please visit our website, www.garethstevens.com. For a free color catalog of all our high-quality books, call toll free 1-800-542-2595 or fax 1-877-542-2596.

Library of Congress Cataloging-in-Publication Data

Harasymiw, Mark.
Termites / by Mark Harasymiw.
p. cm. — (Animals of mass destruction)
Includes index.
ISBN 978-1-4824-1042-6 (pbk.)
ISBN 978-1-4824-1041-9 (6-pack)
ISBN 978-1-4824-1043-3 (library binding)
1. Termites — Juvenile literature. I. Harasymiw, Mark. II. Title.
QL529.H47 2015
595.7—d23

First Edition

Published in 2015 by
Gareth Stevens Publishing
111 East 14th Street, Suite 349
New York, NY 10003

Copyright © 2015 Gareth Stevens Publishing

Designer: Andrea Davison-Bartolotta
Editor: Therese Shea

Photo credits: Cover, p. 1 (main) iStock/Thinkstock; cover, p. 1 (inset) smuay/Shutterstock.com; series art (all textured backgrounds, yellow striped line) Elisanth/Shutterstock.com; series art (caption boxes) Fatseyeva/Shutterstock.com; series art (red boxes) Tracie Andrews/Shutterstock.com; p. 4 Morley Read/iStock/Thinkstock; pp. 4–5 © iStockphoto.com/Atelopus; p. 6 somyot pattana/Shutterstock.com; pp. 6–7, 9 (inset) wonderisland/Shutterstock.com; pp. 8–9 AlessandroZocc/Shutterstock.com; pp. 10–11 Decha Thapanya/Shutterstock.com; pp. 12–13 © iStockphoto.com/randimal; pp. 14–15 Smith Chetanachan/iStock/Thinkstock; pp. 16–17 Wildnerpix/iStock/Thinkstock; p. 18 Norman Reid/iStock/Thinkstock; pp. 18–19 Janette Asche/Flickr/Getty Images; pp. 20–21 Eugene Tochilin/Hemera/Thinkstock; p. 22 mrkon/iStock/Thinkstock; p. 23 (termite) defun/iStock/Thinkstock; p. 23 (ant) Patrick Foto/Shutterstock.com; p. 23 (main) chartcameraman/Shutterstock.com; p. 24 Chokniti Khongchum/Shutterstock.com; pp. 24–25 Rudy Umans/Shutterstock.com; pp. 26, 26–27 Ali Mufti/Shutterstock.com; p. 28 vovan/Shutterstock.com; pp. 28–29 Julie Fletcher/Flickr/Getty Images.

Printed in the United States of America

CPSIA compliance information: Batch #CS15GS: For further information contact Gareth Stevens, New York, New York at 1-800-542-2595.

CONTENTS

Words in the glossary appear in **bold** type the first time they are used in the text.

TERRIBLE TERMITES

Termites are a type of insect that lives in groups, or colonies, of hundreds, thousands, or even millions. A termite's favorite food is wood. This isn't a problem for people when termites are in the wild. However, when termites think someone's house is a source of food, they can cause big problems.

Termites don't only eat the wood of the house. They also eat wood furniture, sheds, fences, and even telephone poles! As long as it's made out of wood, termites will eat it!

Chew On This!

About $2 billion are spent each year in the United States to protect homes from termites.

As you can see, termites never dine alone!

LIFESTYLE OF THE TINY AND HUNGRY

Termites are social insects. That means they live in colonies like bees and ants do. And like bees and ants, each termite belongs to a group, or caste, in its colony. For termites, these castes include **reproductives**, soldiers, and workers.

The reproductives are the kings and queens, the termites that produce new termites for the colony. The soldiers protect the colony from enemy insects. Worker termites make nests, dig tunnels, gather food, and care for the young.

soldier termite

Chew On This!

While workers and soldiers only live 2 to 5 years, kings and queens can live up to 70 years!

In this image, workers are taking care of the queen. As you can see, she's much bigger than the others in the colony.

ROYAL TERMITES

Like almost all insects, termites begin their life cycle as eggs. When they hatch, they're wormlike **larvae** that grow into **nymphs**. After the nymph stage, termites join their caste. The reproductives have wings at first and are sometimes called alates (AY-layts).

A group of alates in the air is called a swarm. When a male and female find each other, they land, lose their wings, find a shelter, and **mate**. The new queen begins laying eggs and takes care of the young with the king.

Chew On This!

In some kinds, or species, of termites, the queen can be 4.3 inches (11 cm) long! She needs to be that size because the termite queen lays thousands of eggs a day.

Termite Life Cycle

queen

eggs

king

nymph

alates

soldier

(winged reproductives)

worker

Separate termite colonies may send out reproductives at the same time, so the alates have a better chance of meeting a mate.

SOLDIERS: DEFENDERS

Some termite young will grow to be soldiers. The job of the soldier termite is to guard the nest from enemies, which are mostly ants and other termites. Soldiers are usually about 0.75 inch (1.9 cm) long.

Soldier termites are armed with "**weapons**" to help them with their duties. They have large heads and strong **mandibles** to fight. Soldier termites of some species can even produce a sticky or poisonous liquid from their head to drive away enemies!

Chew On This!

The mandibles of a soldier termite are quite deadly. They open and close like scissors and can remove body parts from other insects!

This soldier termite is guarding the workers.

← mandibles

WORKERS: DESTROYERS

The termite group with the most members is the worker caste. As you might expect, workers do most of the work! This includes making and repairing the nest and caring for eggs and nymphs.

The other types of termites don't feed themselves. The workers have to provide food for the whole colony. Worker termites search for food, eat it, and provide it to the others by regurgitating it, or throwing up. The worker caste is mostly responsible for the great harm, or damage, that termites can do.

Chew On This!

The workers and soldiers of most species of termites lack both wings and eyes!

New queens and kings feed themselves, but after they have workers like this in the colony, they depend on them for food.

WHAT'S ON THE MENU?

Termites eat wood, grass, leaves, and other plant matter. In these are a **substance** called cellulose that termites are unable to **digest** by themselves. However, they have tiny living things inside their body that turn the cellulose into food they can digest.

All termites have bacteria inside them, but some types have tiny creatures called protozoa, too. Termite nymphs don't have these tiny creatures. Older termites make a special food and feed it to the young termites to pass on the creatures.

Chew On This!

Termites sometimes eat dead or injured termites in order to get **nutrients** that they can't get from wood!

14

Termites can turn a solid piece of wood into a home full of holes!

TERMITE COLONIES

Termites mainly build their nests in or around wood. Some termites make their nests in the stumps and branches of living trees. Other termites build nests in wood that's buried underground. These underground, or subterranean, termites also dig tunnels through soil to other sources of wood.

If the termite nest is open to the outside, as on a tree, termite workers make walls. They use a mixture including chewed wood and spit! This matter is called carton, and it can be thin and papery or hard and wood-like.

Chew On This!

Termites also construct their nests in buildings, chewing their living areas into walls or even into wooden furniture!

As you can see, termites don't have a fear of heights. They'll build their nests in high tree branches.

TERMITE MOUNDS

Some species of termites make huge shelters for their colonies called mounds. These can be shaped like domes or like cones and have several rooms, or galleries, inside.

Some African species make mounds up to 30 feet (9.1 m) tall. The termites that build these huge mounds are the type that grow **fungus** inside their colony for food. This fungus only grows at certain temperatures. The shape of the mound helps air move through the nest to keep the fungus at the right temperature.

Termite mounds can also be a home to other animals, including lizards, snakes, and birds! Termite mounds are found in Africa, Australia, and South America.

CONTROL AND PREVENTION

Termites can be very tricky to find, because they live underground or in the wood of a home's walls. However, people building a house can take action to keep termites away. One way is to put poisons and other matter in the ground under the house to drive back termites or even kill them.

Also, some houses are built so that their wood parts don't touch soil where termites might be exploring for food. Many termites like wet conditions, so keeping a house dry and free of leaks is an important part of fighting these insects, too.

Chew On This!

Some builders put a layer of sand underneath a house to keep away termites. Termites are unable to dig tunnels through sand.

If termites can't chew through an object, they might build tubes like these to protect them as they crawl to food.

TERMITES ARE *NOT* ANTS

If you see some chewed wood near or in your house, you might wonder if the cause is termites or carpenter ants. If you look closely at an ant and a termite next to each other, you can tell the difference. Both termites and ants have **antennae**. However, an ant's antennae are bent, while a termite's antennae are straight.

Both ant and termite alates have two sets of wings. However, the ant alate's sets of wings are different sizes, while the termite alate's wings are the same size.

cockroach

Chew On This!

Ants and termites aren't closely related. Termites' closest relatives are cockroaches.

Another difference between these two insects is the size of their middle section. An ant's middle section is thinner.

termite alate

ant alate

EXTERMINATE!

It takes years for termites to do serious damage to a house. However, if you do find you have termites in your house, you should call an **exterminator**.

Exterminators leave wood or cardboard soaked in poison near the termites. A worker termite who finds this deadly food will bring it back to the colony and share it, killing many termites. If exterminators know where a nest is, they can pump termite poison directly into the nest, killing the insects inside.

ants attacking a termite

Chew On This!

In the wild, termite predators such as ants, spiders, and larger insects can control termite populations.

Another way an exterminator attacks termites in a house is by covering the house with a tent and filling it with poisonous gas!

TERMITE INVADERS

About 70 years ago, a species of termites came to the United States from east Asia. Called Formosan termites, they're even more damaging than **native** termites. Unlike native termites whose colonies contain thousands of individuals, Formosan colonies have millions of hungry termites.

New Orleans, Louisiana, is having trouble with Formosan termites. These insects have been causing about $300 million worth of damage a year in the city by eating historic buildings and trees.

Chew On This!

Unlike most other termites, when Formosan termites are hungry or thirsty, they'll chew through cement, brick, or plastic to get to food and water.

Native termite colonies usually eat about 7 pounds (3.2 kg) of wood a year. Formosan colonies can eat 1,000 pounds (454 kg) of wood a year!

TERMITES AREN'T ALL BAD!

When they're not munching on your house or your wooden furniture, termites can be helpful. In the wild, they eat rotting and dead wood that might just pile up on the ground.

With the help of the bacteria and protozoa in their guts, termites recycle wood into matter that gives soil nutrients so new plants can grow. Animals might need these plants as sources of food. So, thanks in large part to termites, you can enjoy a walk through a healthy forest.

Termites have been on this planet for over 200 million years!

GLOSSARY

antennae: feelers on the head of some animals. The singular of "antennae" is "antenna."

digest: to break down food inside the body so that the body can use it

exterminator: a person who is an expert at removing insects or other small creatures from a building

fungus: a living thing that is somewhat like a plant, but doesn't make its own food, have leaves, or have a green color. Fungi include molds and mushrooms.

larvae: bugs in an early life stage that have a wormlike form. The singular form is "larva."

mandible: a mouthpart of insects or arachnids used to bite or hold food

mate: to come together to make babies. Also, one of two animals that come together to make babies.

native: born and living in a place

nutrient: something a living thing needs to grow and stay alive

nymph: the larva of some insects that looks somewhat like an adult and grows into an adult

reproductive: a social insect that makes babies

substance: matter, stuff, something

weapon: something used to fight an enemy

FOR MORE INFORMATION

Books

George, Lynn. *Termites: Mound Builders*. New York, NY: PowerKids Press, 2011.

Jackson, Cari. *Bugs That Destroy*. New York, NY: Marshall Cavendish Benchmark, 2009.

Telford, Carole, and Rod Theodorou. *Through a Termite City*. Chicago, IL: Heinemann Library, 2006.

Websites

How Termites Work
science.howstuffworks.com/zoology/insects-arachnids/termite.htm
Read about how you can tell if termites are in your house and causing damage.

Termite
www.animalplanet.com/insects/termite-info.htm
Read more about termites and how to control them.

INDEX